God's Little Instruction Book III

Even More Inspirational Wisdom on how
to live a happy and fulfilled life.

Honor Books

God's Little Instruction Book III
ISBN 1-56292-265-3
Copyright © 1997 by Honor Books, Inc.
PO Box 55388
Tulsa, OK 74155
2nd Printing

Introduction

Why another book of quotations, you say? Well, as Isaac D'Israeli said, "The wisdom of the wise and the experience of ages may be preserved by quotation." Therefore, in order to do our part in preserving wisdom and experience we are happy to present to you *God's Little Instruction Book III*.

Ralph Waldo Emerson said, "Next to the originator of a good sentence is the first quoter of it." You will find here the same type of inspirational quotes and nuggets of wisdom contained in *God's Little Instruction Book* and *God's Little Instruction Book II*. And although we may not be the first quoters of the enclosed "sentences" we are perpetuating the practice of quoting, adding of course, the standard by which we measure all wisdom–God's Word.

Winston Churchill said, "It is a good thing for an uneducated man to read books of quotations." We are not presuming that *you* are uneducated, but you surely know *someone* who is. To those authors, speakers, statesmen, businessmen, etc., who are quoted herein, we say, "Thank you." And they would most likely say "You're welcome," because according to Benjamin Franklin, "Nothing gives an author so much pleasure as to find his works respectfully quoted by other learned authors."

We hope you will add *God's Little Instruction Book III* to your treasured collection of favorites.

Why is it that there is never enough time to do a job right, but always time enough to do it over?

The plans of the diligent lead surely to plenty, but those of everyone who is hasty, surely to poverty.
Proverbs 21:5 NKJV

Prayer should be the key of the morning and the lock of the night.

It is good to praise the Lord...to proclaim your love in the morning and your faithfulness at night.
Psalm 92:1,2

If at first you don't succeed, try hard work.

*Hard work always pays off; mere talk puts
no bread on the table.*
Proverbs 14:23 The Message

It is far more impressive when others discover your good qualities without your help.

Let another man praise thee, and not thine own mouth; a stranger, and not thine own lips.
Proverbs 27:2 KJV

Even if you're on the right track, you'll get run over if you just sit there.

So you see, it isn't enough just to have faith.
You must also do good to prove that you have it.
Faith that doesn't show itself by good works is
no faith at all—it is dead and useless.
James 2:17 TLB

Great thoughts reduced to practice become great acts.

Was not Abraham our father justified by works when he offered Isaac his son on the altar? Do you see that faith was working together with his works, and by works faith was made perfect?
James 2:21,22 NKJV

I have always thought the actions of men the best interpreters of their thoughts.

As he thinketh in his heart, so is he.
Proverbs 23:7 KJV

Keep away from people who try to belittle your ambitions. Small people always do that, but the really great people make you feel that you, too, can become great.

Blessed is the man that walketh not in the counsel of the ungodly, nor standeth in the way of sinners, nor sitteth in the seat of the scornful.
Psalm 1:1

Weakness of attitude becomes weakness of character.

And do not be conformed to this world, but be transformed by the renewing of your mind, that you may prove what is that good and acceptable and perfect will of God.
Romans 12:2 NKJV

Most men believe that it would benefit them if they could get a little from those who have more. How much more would it benefit them if they would learn a little from those who know more.

How much better to get wisdom than gold!
Proverbs 16:16 NKJV

How much pain have cost us the evils which have never happened!

Who of you by worrying can add a single hour to his life?
Matthew 6:27

You never saw a fish on the wall with its mouth shut.

The wise in heart accept commands,
but a chattering fool comes to ruin.
Proverbs 10:8

It is right to be contented with what we have, never with what we are.

I have learned how to get along happily
whether I have much or little.
Philippians 4:11 TLB

Anyone who has never made a mistake has never tried anything new.

Forgetting what is behind and straining toward what is ahead, I press on toward the goal.
Philippians 3:13,14

You see things; and you say,
"Why?" But I dream things
that never were; and I say,
"Why not?"

Without faith it is impossible to please God.
Hebrews 11:6

You can't hold a man down without staying down with him.

The man who sets a trap for others will get caught in it himself.
Proverbs 26:27 TLB

What is a cynic? A man who knows the price of everything, and the value of nothing.

OSCAR WILDE

The mind of sinful man is death, but the mind controlled by the Spirit is life and peace.
Romans 8:6

It is impossible to enjoy idling thoroughly unless one has plenty of work to do.

By the seventh day God had finished the work he had been doing; so on the seventh day he rested from all his work.
Genesis 2:2

Isolation is the worst possible counselor.

Where there is no counsel, the people fall;
but in the multitude of counselors there is safety.
Proverbs 11:14 NKJV

Dreaming about a thing in order to do it properly is right; but dreaming about it when we should be doing it is wrong.

He who gathers crops in summer is a wise son, but he who sleeps during harvest is a disgraceful son.
Proverbs 10:5

I will study and prepare myself and then someday my chance will come.

Let us not become weary in doing good, for at the proper time we will reap a harvest if we do not give up.
Galatians 6:9

A poor man is not that one without a cent. A poor man is that one without a dream.

The intelligent man is always open to new ideas.
In fact, he looks for them.
Proverbs 18:15 TLB

The secret to being tiresome is to tell everything.

Even dunces who keep quiet are thought to be wise.
Proverbs 17:28 The Message

Every human being is intended
to have a character of his own;
to be what no other is, and to
do what no other can do.

For we are His workmanship, created in Christ Jesus
for good works, which God prepared beforehand
that we should walk in them.
Ephesians 2:10 NKJV

There is no security in life, only opportunity.

And we know that in all things God works
for the good of those who love him.
Romans 8:28

A pessimist is one who makes difficulties of his opportunities; an optimist is one who makes opportunities of his difficulties.

If God is for us, who can be against us?
Romans 8:31

The most untutored person with passion is more persuasive than the most eloquent without.

For I know your eagerness to help...your enthusiasm has stirred most of them to action.
2 Corinthians 9:2

By perseverance, the snail reached the Ark.

He who works his land will have abundant food,
but he who chases fantasies lacks judgment.
Proverbs 12:11

We can be knowledgeable
with another man's knowledge,
but we cannot be wise with
another man's wisdom.

If any of you lacks wisdom, he should ask God,
who gives generously to all, without finding fault,
and it will be given to him.
James 1:5

A barking dog is often more useful than a sleeping lion.

Anyone who is among the living has hope —
even a live dog is better off than a dead lion!
Ecclesiastes 9:4

One man that has a mind and knows it can always beat ten men who haven't and don't.

I can do all things through Christ who strengthens me.
Philippians 4:13 NKJV

Chance favors prepared minds.

Wise men store up knowledge,
but the mouth of a fool invites ruin.
Proverbs 10:14

Sin has many tools, but a lie is the handle which fits them all.

A lying tongue hates those it hurts,
and a flattering mouth works ruin.
Proverbs 26:28

Don't be "consistent," but be simply true.

Simply let your 'Yes' be 'Yes,' and your 'No,' 'No';
anything beyond this comes from the evil one.
Matthew 5:37

It is a mistake to look too far ahead. Only one link of the chain of destiny can be handled at a time.

You do not even know what will happen tomorrow.
What is your life? You are a mist that appears
for a little while and then vanishes.
James 4:14

There are dreamers and there are planners; the planners make their dreams come true.

But do you not know, O foolish man,
that faith without works is dead.
James 2:20 NKJV

Nothing is so contagious as
an example. We never do great
good or great evil without bringing
about more of the same on the
part of others.

Follow my example, as I follow the example of Christ.
1 Corinthians 11:1

You can make more friends in two months by becoming interested in other people than you can in two years by trying to get other people interested in you.

Love one another with brotherly affection—
as members of one family—giving precedence
and showing honor to one another.
Romans 12:10 AMP

Those who do not plan for the future will have to live through it anyway.

Teach us to number our days aright, that we may gain a heart of wisdom.
Psalm 90:12

From what we get, we can make a living; from what we give, however, makes a life.

One man gives freely, yet gains even more; another withholds unduly, but comes to poverty.
Proverbs 11:24

It is better to give than to lend, and it costs about the same.

But love your enemies, do good to them,
and lend to them without expecting to get
anything back. Then your reward will be great.
Luke 6:35

A great leader never sets himself above his followers except in carrying responsibilities.

And being found in appearance as a man,
he humbled himself and became obedient
to death — even death on a cross!
Philippians 2:8

I don't think much of a man who is not wiser today than he was yesterday.

Study to show thyself approved unto God,
a workman that needeth not to be ashamed,
rightly dividing the word of truth.
2 Timothy 2:15 KJV

Live so that you wouldn't be ashamed to sell the family parrot to the town gossip.

What you have said in the dark will be heard in the daylight, and what you have whispered in the ear in the inner rooms will be proclaimed from the roofs.
Luke 12:3

The greatest pleasure in life is doing what people say you cannot do.

For with God nothing is ever impossible.
Luke 1:37 AMP

We have committed the Golden Rule to memory. Let us now commit it to life.

So in everything, do to others what you would have them do to you.
Matthew 7:12

Pennies do not come from heaven – they have to be earned here on earth.

*From the fruit of his lips a man is filled with good things
as surely as the work of his hands rewards him.*
Proverbs 12:14

Patience serves as a protection against wrongs
as clothes do against cold. For if you put
on more clothes as the cold increases,
it will have no power to hurt you. So in
like manner you must grow in patience
when you meet with great wrongs,
and they will be powerless to vex you.

But let patience have her perfect work, that ye
may be perfect and entire, wanting nothing.
James 1:4 KJV

There is no royal road to anything.
One thing at a time, and all things
in succession. That which grows
slowly endures.

*We do not want you to become lazy, but to
imitate those who through faith and patience
inherit what has been promised.*
Hebrews 6:12

Diligence is the greatest of teachers.

Keep thy heart with all diligence;
for out of it are the issues of life.
Proverbs 4:23 KJV

Here is the test to find whether your mission on earth is finished: If you're alive, it isn't.

For as the days of a tree, so will be the days of my people;
my chosen ones will long enjoy the works of their hands.
Isaiah 65:22

The greatest mistake you can make in life is to be continually fearing you will make one.

Be strong and courageous. Do not be afraid or terrified because of them, for the LORD your God goes with you; he will never leave you nor forsake you.
Deuteronomy 31:6

You have reached the pinnacle of success as soon as you become uninterested in money, compliments, or publicity.

Do nothing out of selfish ambition or vain conceit, but in humility consider others better than yourselves.
Philippians 2:3

Try not to become a man of success, but rather a man of virtue.

A good name is more desirable than great riches; to be esteemed is better than silver or gold.
Proverbs 22:1

Let no feeling of discouragement prey upon you, and in the end you are sure to succeed.

The Lord himself goes before you and will be with you; he will never leave you nor forsake you. Do not be afraid; do not be discouraged.
Deuteronomy 31:8

Men are not influenced by things, but by their thoughts about things.

Finally, brothers, whatever is true, whatever is noble, whatever is right, whatever is pure, whatever is lovely, whatever is admirable—if anything is excellent or praiseworthy—think about such things.
Philippians 4:8

Short as life is, we make it still shorter by the careless waste of time.

Man is like a breath; his days are like a fleeting shadow.
Psalm 144:4

Vision is the art of seeing things invisible.

By faith, he [Abraham] left Egypt, not fearing the king's anger; he persevered because he saw him who is invisible.
Hebrews 11:27

Wisdom begins with sacrifice of immediate pleasures for long range purposes.

Make level paths for your feet and take only ways that are firm. Do not swerve to the right or the left; keep your foot from evil.
Proverbs 4:26,27

Study without reflection is a waste of time; reflection without study is dangerous.

Do not let this Book of the Law depart from your mouth; meditate on it day and night, so that you may be careful to do everything written in it. Then you will be prosperous and successful.
Joshua 1:8

To know is not to be wise....
There is no fool so great a fool
as a knowing fool. But to know
how to use knowledge is
to have wisdom.

The fear of the Lord is the beginning of knowledge,
but fools despise wisdom and discipline.
Proverbs 1:7

Better to light a candle than to curse the darkness.

The eye is the lamp of the body. If your eyes are good, your whole body will be full of light.
Matthew 6:22

What comes with ease, goes with ease.

Dishonest money dwindles away, but he who gathers money little by little makes it grow.
Proverbs 13:11

Render more service than that for which you are paid and you will soon be paid for more than you render. This is *The law of increasing returns.*

Remember this: Whoever sows sparingly will also reap sparingly, and whoever sows generously will also reap generously.
2 Corinthians 9:6

Those who complain the most usually work the least.

Do everything without complaining or arguing.
Philippians 2:14

We cannot be guilty of a greater act of uncharitableness, than to interpret the afflictions which befall our neighbors, as punishment and judgments.

Stop judging by mere appearances,
and make a right judgment.
John 7:24

Aspiration shows us the goal and the distance to it; inspiration encourages with a view to how far we have come. Aspiration gives us the map of the journey; inspiration furnishes the music to keep us marching.

Then the Lord answered me and said,
"Record the vision and inscribe it on tablets.
That the one who reads it may run."
Habakkuk 2:2 NASB

Understanding is the reward of faith. Therefore seek not to understand that thou mayest believe, but believe that thou mayest understand.

*Jesus answered, "The work of God is this:
to believe in the one he has sent."*
John 6:29

Amid the greatest difficulties of my Administration, when I could not see any other resort, I would place my whole reliance in God, knowing that all would go well, and that He would decide for the right.

Cast your cares on the Lord and he will sustain you.
Psalm 55:22

A true friend never gets in your way unless you happen to be going down.

If one falls down, his friend can help him up. But pity the man who falls and has no one to help him up!
Ecclesiastes 4:10

Other books were given for our information, the Bible was given for our transformation.

Do not conform any longer to the pattern of this world, but be transformed by the renewing of your mind.
Romans 12:2

We must adjust to changing times and still hold to unchanging principles.

The word of the Lord stands forever.
1 Peter 1:25

The seen is the changing, the unseen is the unchanging.

So we fix our eyes not on what is seen, but on what is unseen. For what is seen is temporary, but what is unseen is eternal.
2 Corinthians 4:18

The trouble with modern civilization is that we so often mistake respectability for character.

Man looks at the outward appearance,
but the Lord looks at the heart.
1 Samuel 16:7

One of the disconcerting facts about the spiritual life is that God takes you at your word.

*Whatever your lips utter you must be sure to do,
because you made your vow freely to the Lord
your God with your own mouth.*
Deuteronomy 23:23

Kindness has converted more people than zeal, science, or eloquence.

Or do you show contempt for the riches of his kindness, tolerance and patience, not realizing that God's kindness leads you toward repentance?
Romans 2:4

A quiet conscience sleeps in thunder.

Paul looked straight at the Sanhedrin and said, "My brothers, I have fulfilled my duty to God in all good conscience to this day."
Acts 23:1

Conformity is the jailer of freedom and the enemy of growth.

Then you will know the truth,
and the truth will set you free.
John 8:32

All too often a clear conscience is merely the result of a bad memory.

These liars have lied so well and for so long that they've lost their capacity for truth.
1 Timothy 4:2 The Message

Courage is rightly esteemed
the first of human qualities,
because...it is the quality
which guarantees all others.

*Be strong and courageous...for the Lord your God
will be with you wherever you go.*
Joshua 1:9

Courage is never to let your actions be influenced by your fears.

For God has not given us a spirit of fear,
but of power and of love and of a sound mind.
2 Timothy 1:7 NKJV

Despair is the sin which cannot find–because it will not look for it–forgiveness.

If we confess our sins, he is faithful and just and will forgive us our sins and purify us from all unrighteousness.
1 John 1:9

There are enough targets to aim at without firing at each other.

Be kind and compassionate to one another, forgiving each other, just as in Christ God forgave you.
Ephesians 4:32

You always pass failure on the way to success.

And we know that all things work together for good to those who love God, to those who are the called according to His purpose.
Romans 8:28 NKJV

There is nothing final about a mistake, except its being taken as final.

The steps of a good man are ordered by the Lord...
Though he fall, he shall not be utterly cast down.
Psalm 37:23,24 KJV

We are never defeated unless we give up on God.

*In all these things we are more than conquerors
through him who loved us.*
Romans 8:37

Faith furnishes prayer with wings, without which it cannot soar to Heaven.

Whatever you ask for in prayer, believe that you have received it, and it will be yours.
Mark 11:24

Faith is not a dam which prevents
the flow of the river of reason and
thought; it is a levee which prevents
unreason from flooding
the countryside.

*Without weakening in his faith, he [Abraham] faced
the fact that his body was as good as dead.*
Romans 4:19

An ounce of parent is worth a pound of the clergy.

Train a child in the way he should go, and when he is old he will not turn from it.
Proverbs 22:6

Hope arouses, as nothing else can arouse, a passion for the possible.

Praise be to the God and Father of our Lord Jesus Christ!
In his great mercy he has given us new birth into
a living hope through the resurrection of Jesus Christ
from the dead.
1 Peter 1:3

It is the heart that is not yet
sure of its God that is afraid
to laugh in His presence.

Let us then approach the throne of grace with confidence,
so that we may receive mercy and find grace to help
us in our time of need.
Hebrews 4:16

Marriage is that relation between man and woman in which the independence is equal, the dependence mutual, and the obligation reciprocal.

Wives, understand and support your husbands...
Husbands, go all out in love for your wives.
Colossians 3:18,19 The Message

The goal in marriage is not to think alike, but to think together.

For this reason a man will leave his father and mother and be united to his wife, and the two will become one flesh.
Ephesians 5:31

Money \ˈmə-nē \ n.,
A blessing that is of no advantage to us excepting when we part with it.

*Each man should give what he has decided in his heart
to give, not reluctantly or under compulsion,
for God loves a cheerful giver.*
2 Corinthians 9:7

Obedience is the "virtue-making virtue."

Does the Lord delight in burnt offerings and sacrifices as much as in obeying the voice of the Lord? To obey is better than sacrifice.
1 Samuel 15:22

All sunshine makes a desert.

*Consider it pure joy, my brothers, whenever you face
trials of many kinds, because you know that the
testing of your faith develops perseverance.*
James 1:2,3

Patience is the companion of wisdom.

Let us run with patience the race that is set before us.
Hebrews 12:1 KJV

If I had eight hours to chop down a tree, I'd spend six sharpening my ax.

Be prepared in season and out of season.
2 Timothy 4:2

What is the use of praying if at the very moment of prayer we have so little confidence in God that we are busy planning our own kind of answer to our prayer?

Do not be anxious about anything, but in everything, by prayer and petition, with thanksgiving, present your requests to God.
Philippians 4:6

Our motive for prayer must be the divine will, not our own.

Therefore do not be foolish, but understand what the Lord's will is.
Ephesians 5:17

I do not feel obliged to believe that the same God who has endowed us with sense, reason, and intellect has intended us to forgo their use.

Each one should be fully convinced in his own mind.
Romans 14:5

Self-reform is the answer to world-reform.

Each of us will give an account of himself to God.
Romans 14:12

The worst cliques are those which consist of one man.

Do not think of yourself more highly than you ought.
Romans 12:3

In taking revenge a man is but even with his enemy; but in passing it over, he is superior.

Do not repay anyone evil for evil. Be careful to do what is right in the eyes of everybody.
Romans 12:17

Let not the nation count wealth as wealth; let it count righteousness as wealth.

Blessed is the nation whose God is the Lord.
Psalm 33:12

The secrets of success are a good wife and a steady job. My wife told me.

*He who finds a wife finds what is good
and receives favor from the Lord.*
Proverbs 18:22

The power of a man's virtue should not be measured by his special efforts, but by his ordinary doing.

Live such good lives among the pagans that, though they accuse you of doing wrong, they may see your good deeds and glorify God.
1 Peter 2:12

In this world it is not what we take up, but what we give up, that makes us rich.

Give, and it will be given to you. A good measure,
pressed down, shaken together and running over,
will be poured into your lap.
Luke 6:38

It is not a crime to be rich,
nor a virtue to be poor....
the sin lies in hoarding wealth
and keeping it from circulating
freely to all who need it.

*You will be made rich in every way so that you
can be generous on every occasion...your generosity
will result in thanksgiving to God.*
2 Corinthians 9:11

The created world is but a small parenthesis in eternity.

So we fix our eyes not on what is seen,
but on what is unseen. For what is seen is
temporary, but what is unseen is eternal.
2 Corinthians 4:18

Money is like promises—easier made than kept.

Whoever trusts in his riches will fall, but the righteous will thrive like a green leaf.
Proverbs 11:28

Money is of no value;
it cannot spend itself.
All depends on the skill
of the spender.

Moreover it is required in stewards
that one be found faithful.
1 Corinthians 4:2 NKJV

The squeaky wheel doesn't always get greased; it often gets replaced.

Let your conversation be always full of grace, seasoned with salt, so that you may know how to answer everyone.
Colossians 4:6

No generalization is wholly true, not even this one.

My mouth speaks what is true,
for my lips detest wickedness.
Proverbs 8:7

It thou thinkest twice, before thou speakest once, thou wilt speak twice the better for it.

He who guards his mouth and his tongue
keeps himself from calamity.
Proverbs 21:23

The drops of rain make a hole in the stone not by violence but by oft falling.

Through patience a ruler can be persuaded,
and a gentle tongue can break a bone.
Proverbs 25:15

Our grand business in life is not to see what lies dimly at a distance, but to do what lies clearly at hand.

Whatever your hand finds to do, do it with all your might.
Ecclesiastes 9:10

The world is moving so fast these days that the man who says it can't be done is generally interrupted by someone doing it.

For nothing is impossible with God.
Luke 1:37

Every tomorrow has two handles.
You can take hold of the handle
of anxiety or the handle of
enthusiasm. Upon your choice
so will be the day.

*In the morning, O Lord, you hear my voice; in the morning
I lay my requests before you and wait in expectation.*
Psalm 5:3

The last of the human freedoms is to choose one's attitude in any given set of circumstances.

Whatever is true...noble...right...pure...lovely...admirable...
excellent or praiseworthy — think about such things.
Philipians 4:8

Example is not the main thing in influencing others. It is the only thing.

Christ suffered for you, leaving you an example,
that you should follow in his steps.
1 Peter 2:21

Genius is nothing but a greater aptitude for patience.

*Imitate those who through faith and patience
inherit what has been promised.*
Hebrews 6:12

Blessed is the man who, having nothing to say, abstains from giving in words evidence of the fact.

The tongue is a small part of the body, but it makes great boasts. Consider what a great forest is set on fire by a small spark.
James 3:5

Most of man's trouble comes from his inability to be still.

Be still, and know that I am God; I will be exalted among the nations, I will be exalted in the earth.
Psalm 46:10

I don't know why we are in such a hurry to get up when we fall down. You might think we would lie there and rest awhile.

He makes me lie down in green pastures, he leads me beside quiet waters, he restores my soul.
Psalm 23:2,3

Happiness is a dividend on a well-invested life.

When you eat the labor of your hands, You shall be happy, and it shall be well with you.
Psalm 128:2 NKJV

I am not interested in the past.
I am interested in the future,
for that is where I expect to
spend the rest of my life.

*Forgetting what is behind and straining toward what is
ahead, I press on toward the goal to win the prize.*
Philippians 3:13,14

The future is something which everyone reaches at the rate of sixty minutes an hour, whatever he does, whoever he is.

For the revelation awaits an appointed time; it speaks of the end and will not prove false. Though it linger, wait for it; it will certainly come and will not delay.
Habakkuk 2:3

A person may sometimes have a clear conscience simply because his head is empty.

In the last times some in the church will turn away from Christ...their consciences won't even bother them.
1 Timothy 4:2 TLB

A wise man sometimes changes his mind, but a fool never.

The way of a fool seems right to him,
but a wise man listens to advice.
Proverbs 12:15

A leader is a dealer in hope.

A faith and knowledge resting on the hope of eternal life, which God, who does not lie, promised before the beginning of time.
Titus 1:2

We don't need any more leadership training; we need some followership training.

*Anyone who does not take his cross
and follow me is not worthy of me.*
Matthew 10:38

Any plant growing in the wrong place is a "weed."

But in fact God has arranged the parts in the body, every one of them, just as he wanted them to be.
1 Corinthians 12:18

The well of Providence is deep. It's the buckets we bring to it that are small.

Look at the birds of the air...your heavenly Father feeds them. Are you not much more valuable than they?
Matthew 6:26

Whatever you dislike in another person take care to correct in yourself.

Why do you look at the speck of sawdust in your brother's eye and pay no attention to the plank in your own eye?
Matthew 7:3

Honor's a lease for life
to come.

We are looking forward to a new heaven and a new earth,
the home of righteousness.
2 Peter 3:13

Hope is brightest when it dawns from fears.

He has delivered us from such a deadly peril, and he will deliver us. On him we have set our hope that he will continue to deliver us.
2 Corinthians 1:10

Any man may commit a mistake, but none but a fool will continue in it.

Though a righteous man falls seven times, he rises again,
but the wicked are brought down by calamity.
Proverbs 24:16

Gold is the fool's curtain, which hides all his defects from the world.

The wealth of the rich is their fortified city;
they imagine it an unscalable wall.
Proverbs 18:11

Conversation is the vent of character as well as of thought.

For out of the overflow of the heart the mouth speaks. The good man brings good things out of the good stored up in him, and the evil man...out of the evil stored up in him.
Matthew 12:34,35

Every individual has a place to fill
in the world, and is important,
in some respect, whether he
chooses to be so or not.

*For I know the thoughts and plans that I have for you, says
the Lord, thoughts and plans for welfare and peace, and
not for evil, to give you hope in your final outcome.*
Jeremiah 29:11 AMP

Goodness is the only investment that never fails.

But the fruit of the Spirit is love, joy, peace, patience, kindness, goodness, faithfulness, gentleness, self-control; against such things there is no law.
Galatians 5:22,23 NASB

It is what we give up, not what we lay up, that adds to our lasting store.

Do not store up for yourselves treasures on earth...
But store up for yourselves treasures in heaven....
For where your treasure is there your heart will be also.
Matthew 6:19-21

The time to repair the roof is when the sun is shining.

Go to the ant...consider its ways and be wise!
It has no commander...yet it stores its provisions
in summer and gathers its food at harvest.
Proverbs 6:6,8

The men who try to do something and fail are infinitely better than those who try nothing and succeed.

"Take the thousand and give it to the one who
risked the most. And get rid of this 'play-it-safe'
who won't go out on a limb."
Matthew 25:29,30 The Message

No worldly success can compensate for failure in the home.

Children, obey your parents in the Lord, for this is right...And you, fathers, do not provoke your children to wrath, but bring them up in the training and admonition of the Lord.
Ephesians 6:1,4 NKJV

Coming together is a beginning;
keeping together is progress;
working together is success.

How good and pleasant it is when brothers live together
in unity!...For there the LORD bestows his blessing,
even life forevermore.
Psalm 133:1,3

If the journey is long, take only the necessities. This leaves room to acquire the luxuries along the way.

Do not store up for yourselves treasures on earth, where moth and rust destroy, and where thieves break in and steal.
Matthew 6:19

Time is a great teacher, but unfortunately it kills all its pupils.

Take my yoke upon you and learn from me, for I am gentle and humble in heart, and you will find rest for your souls.
Matthew 11:29

Once the game is over, the king and the pawn go back into the same box.

For all can see that wise men die; the foolish and the senseless alike perish and leave their wealth to others.
Psalm 49:10

References

Acknowledgments

We acknowledge and thank the following people for the quotes used in this book: Owen Felltham (6), William Feather (7), Judith S. Martin (8), Will Rogers (9,48), William Hazlitt (10), John Locke (11), Mark Twain (12,29), Albert Einstein (13,18,58), William J.H. Boetcker (14), Thomas Jefferson (15), Sally Berger (16), Sir James Mackintosh (17), George Bernard Shaw (19,35,107), Booker T. Washington (20), Oscar Wilde (21), Jerome K. Jerome (22), Miguel de Unamuno (23), Oswald Chambers (24), Abraham Lincoln (25,47,59,73,102), Henry Ford (26,151), Francois Voltaire (27), Channing (28), Reginald Mansell (30), Francois de La Rochefoucauld (31,41), Charles Spurgeon (32,65), Michel de Montaigne (33), Washington Irving (34), Louis Pasteur (36), Oliver Wendell Holmes (37,38,118), Sir Winston Churchill (39,84), Dale Carnegie (42), Len Fisher (43), Arthur Ashe (44), Philip Gibbs (45), Jules Ormont (46), Walter Bagehot (49), Edwin Markham (50), Margaret Thatcher (51), Leonardo da Vinci (52), J.G. Holland (53), Arabian Proverb (54,67,100,134), Richard Bach (55), Elbert G. Hubbard (56), Dr. Orlando A. Battista (57), Epictetus (60), Victor Hugo (61), Jonathan Swift (62), Louis Finkelstein (63), Confucius (64,109), Chinese Proverb (66), Napoleon Hill (68), Joseph Addison (70), Ralph W. Sockman (71,133), St. Augustine (72,101), Arnold Glasow (74), Jimmy Carter (76), Plato (77), Dorothy Day (79), Mother Teresa (80), Thomas Fuller (81,108), John F. Kennedy

(82,148) Arthur Koestler (85), Hubert van Zeller (86), Theodore Roosevelt (87), Mickey Rooney (88), Phyllis Bottome (89), Ronald Reagan (90), St. John Climacus (91), Fulton J. Sheen (92), Spanish Proverb (93), William Sloane Coffin, Jr. (94), George Macdonald (95), Louis K. Anspacher (96), Robert C. Dodds (97), Ambrose Bierce (98), George J. Haye (99), Thomas Merton (103), D. Laurence Scupoli (104), Galileo (105), Sebastian Miklas (106), Howard Nemerov (110), Blaise Pascal (111,128), Henry Ward Beecher (112), Charles Fillmore (113), Thomas Browne (114), Josh Billings (115), Ralph Waldo Emerson (116,144), John Peers (117), William Penn (119), Lucretius (120), Thomas Carlyle (121), Harry Emerson Fosdick (122), Victor Frankl (124), Albert Schweitzer (125), Benjamin Franklin (126), George Eliot (127), Max Eastman (129), Duncan Stuart (130), Charles F. Kettering (131), C.S. Lewis (132), Napoleon Bonaparte (135), Maureen Carroll (136), Farmer's Almanac (137), Mary Webb (138), Sprat (139), Samuel Butler (140), Sir Walter Scott (141), Cicero (142), Feltham (143), Hawthorne (145), Hosea Ballou (147), Llyod Jones (149), Hector Berloiz (153), Italian Proverb (154).

Additional copies of this book and other titles in the *God's Little Instruction Book* series are available at your local bookstore.

God's Little Instruction Book
God's Little Instruction Book, II
God's Little Instruction Book for Mom
God's Little Instruction Book for Dad
God's Little Instruction Book for Graduates
God's Little Instruction Book for Students

Tulsa, Oklahoma